Easy and Fast Air Fryer Recipes

Learn How to Prepare Easy, Fast, Tasty and Healthy Recipes with Your Air Fryer on a Budget

Linda Wang

© **Copyright 2021 by Linda Wang - All rights reserved.**

The content contained within this book may not be reproduced, duplicated or transmitted without direct written permission from the author or the publisher.
Under no circumstances will any blame or legal responsibility be held against the publisher, or author, for any damages, reparation, or monetary loss due to the information contained within this book. Either directly or indirectly.

Legal Notice:
This book is copyright protected. This book is only for personal use. You cannot amend, distribute, sell, use, quote or paraphrase any part, or the content within this book, without the consent of the author or publisher.

Disclaimer Notice:
Please note the information contained within this document is for educational and entertainment purposes only. All effort has been executed to present accurate, up to date, and reliable, complete information. No warranties of any kind are declared or implied. Readers acknowledge that the author is not engaging in the rendering of legal, financial, medical or professional advice. The content within this book has been derived from various sources. Please consult a licensed professional before attempting any techniques outlined in this book.
By reading this document, the reader agrees that under no circumstances is the author responsible for any losses, direct or indirect, which are incurred as a result of the use of information contained within this document, including, but not limited to, — errors, omissions, or inaccuracies.

TABLE OF CONTENTS

INTRODUCTION 1

Zucchini Salad 5

Chicken Burrito 7

Spinach and Olives 9

Delicious Pasta Salad 10

Homemade Mexican Pizza 13

Bok Choy and Butter Sauce 15

Roasted Vegetables Dish 17

Pesto Salmon 19

Lemon Garlic Shrimps 21

Creamy Breaded Shrimp 23

Shrimp Kebabs 25

Scallops with Capers Sauce 27

Crab Cakes 29

Delicious Shrimp recipe 31

Lemon Fish 33

Tomato & Basil Scallops 35

Shrimp and Spaghetti 37

Duck Breast with Figs 39

Gyro Seasoned Chicken 41

Chicken and Yogurt 43

Chicken and Baby Carrots 45

Chicken Fajita Casserole 47

Rotisserie Chicken 49

Mustard Lamb Loin Chops 50

Leg of Lamb with Brussels Sprout 52

Beef Pot Pie 54

Five Spice Pork 56

Beef Roast 58

Paprika Beef 59

Pork Spare Ribs 60

Garlic Lamb Roast 62

Veal, speck, and cheese paupiettes 64

Broccoli Crust Pizza 66

Beef Noodle Soup 68

Tortilla and White Beans Soup 71

Chestnut Soup 73

Pearl Barley Soup 75

Bacon Wrapped Onion Rings. 77

Parmesan Chicken Wings 79

Sponge Ricotta Cake 81

Lemon Blackberries Cake 83

Lemon Bars 85

Coconut Cookies 87

Chocolaty Squares 89

Cherry Pie 91

Pear Delight 93

Butter Donuts 95

Brioche Pudding 96

Lusciously Easy Brownies 97

Espresso Mini Cheesecake 99

NOTES 101

INTRODUCTION

An Air Fryer is a magic revolutionized kitchen appliance that helps you fry with less or even no oil at all. This kind of product applies Rapid Air technology, which offers a new way to fry with less oil. This new invention cooks food through the circulation of superheated air and generates 80% low-fat food. Although the food is fried with less oil, you don't need to worry as the food processed by the Air Fryer still has the same taste like the food fried using the deep-frying method.

This technology uses a superheated element, which radiates heat close to the food and an exhaust fan in its lid to circulate airflow. An Air Fryer ensures that the food processed is cooked completely. The exhaust fan located at the top of the cooking chamber helps the food get the same heating temperature in every part quickly, resulting in a cooked food of better and healthier quality. Besides, cooking with an Air Fryer is also suitable for those individuals which are too busy or do not have enough time. For example, an Air Fryer only needs half a spoonful of oil and takes 10 minutes to serve a medium bowl of crispy French fries.

In addition to serving healthier food, an Air Fryer also provides some other benefits to you. Since an Air Fryer helps you fry using less oil or without oil for some kind of food, it automatically reduces the fat and cholesterol content in food. Indeed, no one will refuse to enjoy fried food without worrying about the greasy and fat content. Having fried food with no guilt is one of the pleasures of life. Besides having low fat and cholesterol, you save some amount of money by consuming oil sparingly, which can be used for other needs. An Air Fryer also can reheat your food. Sometimes, when you have fried leftover and you reheat it, it will usually serve reheated greasy food with some addition of unhealthy reuse oil. Undoubtedly, the saturated fat in the fried food gets worse because of this process. An Air Fryer helps you reheat your food without being afraid of extra oils that the food may absorb. Fried bananas, fish and chips, nuggets, or even fried chicken can be reheated to become as warm and crispy as they were before by using an Air Fryer.

Some people may think that spending some amount of money to buy a fryer is wasteful. I dare to say that they are wrong because an Air Fryer is not only used to fry. It is a sophisticated multi-function appliance since it also helps you to roast chicken, make steak, grill fish, and even bake a cake. With a built-in air filter, an Air Fryer filters the air and saves your kitchen from smoke and grease.

An air Fryer is really a new innovative method of cooking. Grab it fast and welcome to a clean and healthy kitchen.

Zucchini Salad

Preparation Time: 10 minutes

Cooking Time: 25 minutes

Serve: 4

Ingredients:

- 1 lb zucchini, cut into slices
- 1 yellow squash, diced
- 2 tbsp tomato paste
- ½ tbsp tarragon, chopped
- ½ lb carrots, peeled and diced
- 1 tbsp olive oil
- Pepper
- Salt

Directions:

1. In an air fryer baking dish, mix together zucchini, tomato paste, tarragon, squash, carrots, pepper, and salt. Drizzle with olive oil.
2. Place in the air fryer and cook at 400 F for 25 minutes. Stir halfway through.
3. Serve and enjoy.

Nutrition:

Calories 79, Fat 3 g, Carbohydrates 11 g, Sugar 5 g, Protein 2 g, Cholesterol 0 mg

Chicken Burrito

Preparation Time: 15 minutes

Servings: 2

Ingredients:

- 4 chicken breast slices; cooked and shredded
- 2 tortillas
- 1 green bell pepper; sliced
- 1 avocado; peeled, pitted and sliced
- 2 eggs; whisked

- 2 tbsp. cheddar cheese; grated
- 2 tbsp. mild salsa
- Salt and black pepper to taste

Directions:

1. In a bowl, whisk the eggs with the salt and pepper and pour them into a pan that fits your air fryer. Put the pan in the air fryer's basket, cook for 5 minutes at 400°F and transfer the mix to a plate
2. Place the tortillas on a working surface and between them divide the eggs, chicken, bell peppers, avocado and the cheese; roll the burritos
3. Line your air fryer with tin foil, add the burritos and cook them at 300°F for 3-4 minutes. Serve for breakfast, lunch, or dinner!

Spinach and Olives

Preparation Time: 25 minutes

Servings: 4

Ingredients:

- ½ cup tomato puree
- 2 cups black olives, pitted and halved
- 4 cups spinach; torn
- 3 celery stalks; chopped.
- 2 tomatoes; chopped.
- 1 red bell pepper; chopped.
- Salt and black pepper to taste.

Directions:

1. In a pan that fits your air fryer, mix all the ingredients except the spinach, toss, introduce the pan in the air fryer and cook at 370°F for 15 minutes
2. Add the spinach, toss, cook for 5 - 6 minutes more, divide into bowls and serve.

Nutrition:

Calories: 193; Fat: 6g; Fiber: 2g; Carbs: 4g; Protein: 6g

Delicious Pasta Salad

Preparation Time: 2 hours 25 minutes

Servings: 4

Ingredients:

- 4 tomatoes; medium and cut in eighths
- 3 zucchinis; medium sized
- 3 eggplants; small
- 2 bell peppers; any color
- 4 cups large pasta; uncooked in any shape
- 1/2 cup Italian dressing; fat-free
- 1 cup cherry tomatoes; sliced
- 8 tablespoon parmesan; grated
- 2 teaspoon pink Himalayan salt
- 2 tablespoon extra virgin olive oil
- 1 teaspoon basil; dried
- high quality cooking spray

Directions:

1. Wash eggplant; pat it dry and then slice off and discard the stem. Do not peel the eggplant. Slice it into 1/2-inch-thick rounds.

2. Toss the eggplant with one tablespoon of extra virgin olive oil, and put the rounds in the Air Fryer basket.

3. Cook eggplant for 40 minutes at 350 - degrees Fahrenheit. Once it is soft and has no raw taste remaining, set the eggplant aside.

4. Wash the zucchini; pat it dry and then slice off and discard the stem. Do not peel the zucchini. Slice the zucchini into 1/2 -inch rounds.

5. Toss together with extra virgin olive oil, and put it in the Air Fryer basket.

6. Cook zucchini for about 25 minutes at 350 - degrees Fahrenheit. Once it is soft with no raw taste remaining set the zucchini aside.

7. Wash the tomatoes and slice them into eighths. Arrange them in the Air Fryer basket and spray gently with high-quality cooking spray. Roast the tomatoes for 30 minutes at 350 - degrees Fahrenheit. Once they have shrunk and are starting to brown, set them aside.

8. Cook the pasta according to the package's directions, drain them through a colander, and

run them under cold water. Set them aside so they will cool off.

9. Wash the bell peppers; cut them in half, take off the stem and remove the seeds. Rinse under water if you need to, and then pat them dry.

10. Wash the cherry tomatoes and cut them in half.

11. In a large bowl, combine bell peppers and cherry tomatoes. Then, add in the roasted vegetables, cooked pasta, pink Himalayan salt, dressing, chopped basil leaves, and grated parmesan. Mix thoroughly.

12. Set the salad in the fridge to chill and marinade. Serve the salad chilled or at room temperature.

Homemade Mexican Pizza

Preparation Time: 15 minutes

Servings: 2

Ingredients:

- 3/4 cup of refried beans
- 12 frozen beef meatballs; pre-cooked
- 1 cup salsa
- 2 jalapeno peppers; sliced
- 6 whole-wheat pita bread
- 1 cup Colby cheese; shredded
- 1 cup pepper Jack cheese; shredded

Directions:

1. Take a bowl and combine salsa, meatball, jalapeno pepper and beans. Preheat the Air Fryer for 4 minutes at 370 - degrees Fahrenheit.
2. Top the pita with the mixture and sprinkle pepper jack and Colby cheese on top. Bake in Air Fryer for 10 minutes. Serve and enjoy.

Bok Choy and Butter Sauce

Preparation Time: 20 minutes

Servings: 4

Ingredients:

- 2 bok choy heads; trimmed and cut into strips
- 2 tbsp. chicken stock
- 1 tbsp. butter; melted
- 1 tsp. lemon juice
- 1 tbsp. olive oil
- A pinch of salt and black pepper

Directions:

1. In a pan that fits your air fryer, mix all the ingredients, toss, introduce the pan in the air fryer and cook at 380°F for 15 minutes.
2. Divide between plates and serve as a side dish

Nutrition:

Calories: 141; Fat: 3g; Fiber: 2g; Carbs: 4g; Protein: 3g

Roasted Vegetables Dish

Preparation Time: 30 minutes

Servings: 3

Ingredients:

- 1 1/3 cup parsnips [1 small]
- 1 1/3 cup celery [3 – 4 stalks]
- 1 1/3 cup butternut squash [1 small]
- 2 red onions
- 1 tablespoon olive oil
- 1 tablespoon fresh thyme needles
- pepper and salt to taste

Directions:

1. Preheat the Air Fryer to 390 - degrees Fahrenheit.
2. Peel the parsnips and onions. Cut the parsnips and celery into 2 Cm cubes and the onions into wedges.
3. Halve the butternut squash; remove the seeds and cut into cubes. [There's no need to peel it.]
4. Mix the cut vegetables with thyme and olive oil. Season to taste.

5. Place the vegetables into the basket and slide the basket into the Air Fryer.
6. Set the timer for 20 minutes and roast the vegetables until the timer rings and the vegetables are nicely brown and done.
7. Stir the vegetables once while roasting.

Pesto Salmon

Preparation Time: 10 minutes

Cooking Time: 16 minutes

Serve: 4

Ingredients:

- 25 oz salmon fillet
- 1 cup mayonnaise
- 1 tbsp green pesto
- 1/2 oz olive oil
- 2 oz parmesan cheese, grated
- 1 lb fresh spinach
- Pepper
- Salt

Directions:

1. Preheat the air fryer to 370 F.
2. Spray air fryer basket with cooking spray.
3. Season salmon fillet with pepper and salt and place into the air fryer basket.
4. In a bowl, mix together mayonnaise, parmesan cheese, and pesto and spread over the salmon fillet.

5. Cook salmon for 14-16 minutes.
6. Meanwhile, in a pan sauté spinach with olive oil until spinach is wilted, about 2-3 minutes. Season with pepper and salt.
7. Transfer spinach in serving plate and top with cooked salmon.
8. Serve and enjoy.

Nutrition:

Calories 545, Fat 39.6 g, Carbohydrates 9.5 g, Sugar 3.1 g, Protein 43 g, Cholesterol 110 mg

Lemon Garlic Shrimps

Preparation Time: 15 minutes

Cooking Time: 8 minutes

Servings: 2

Ingredients:

- ¾ pound medium shrimp, peeled and deveined
- 1 tablespoon olive oil
- 1½ tablespoons fresh lemon juice
- 1 teaspoon lemon pepper

- ¼ teaspoon paprika
- ¼ teaspoon garlic powder

Directions:

1. Preheat the Air fryer to 400 degrees F and grease an Air fryer basket.
2. Mix lemon juice, olive oil, lemon pepper, paprika and garlic powder in a large bowl.
3. Stir in the shrimp and toss until well combined.
4. Arrange shrimp into the Air fryer basket in a single layer and cook for about 8 minutes.
5. Dish out the shrimp in serving plates and serve warm.

Nutrition:

Calories: 260, Fat: 12.4g, Carbohydrates: 0.3g, Sugar: 0.1g, Protein: 35.6g, Sodium: 619mg

Creamy Breaded Shrimp

Preparation Time: 15 minutes

Cooking Time: 20 minutes

Servings: 3

Ingredients:

- ¼ cup all-purpose flour
- 1 pound shrimp, peeled and deveined
- 1 cup panko breadcrumbs
- ¼ cup sweet chili sauce
- ½ cup mayonnaise
- 1 tablespoon Sriracha sauce

Directions:

1. Preheat the Air fryer to 400 degrees F and grease an Air fryer basket.
2. Place flour in a shallow bowl and mix the mayonnaise, chili sauce, and Sriracha sauce in another bowl.
3. Place the breadcrumbs in a third bowl.
4. Coat each shrimp with the flour, dip into mayonnaise mixture and finally, dredge in the breadcrumbs.

5. Arrange half of the coated shrimps into the Air fryer basket and cook for about 10 minutes.
6. Dish out the coated shrimps onto serving plates and repeat with the remaining mixture.

Nutrition:

Calories: 540, Fat: 18.2g, Carbohydrates: 33.1g, Sugar: 10.6g, Protein: 36.8g, Sodium: 813mg

Shrimp Kebabs

Preparation Time: 15 minutes

Cooking Time: 10 minutes

Servings: 2

Ingredients:

- ¾ pound shrimp, peeled and deveined
- Wooden skewers, presoaked

- 2 tablespoons fresh lemon juice
- 1 tablespoon fresh cilantro, chopped
- 1 teaspoon garlic, minced
- ½ teaspoon ground cumin
- ½ teaspoon paprika
- Salt and ground black pepper, as required

Directions:

1. Preheat the Air fryer to 350 degrees F and grease an Air fryer basket.
2. Mix lemon juice, garlic, and spices in a bowl.
3. Stir in the shrimp and mix to coat well.
4. Thread the shrimp onto presoaked wooden skewers and transfer to the Air fryer basket.
5. Cook for about 10 minutes, flipping once in between.
6. Dish out the mixture onto serving plates and serve garnished with fresh cilantro.

Nutrition:

Calories: 212, Fat: 3.2g, Carbohydrates: 3.9g, Sugar: 0.4g, Protein: 39.1g, Sodium: 497mg

Scallops with Capers Sauce

Preparation Time: 15 minutes

Cooking Time: 6 minutes

Servings: 2

Ingredients:

- 10: 1-ounce sea scallops, cleaned and patted very dry
- 2 tablespoons fresh parsley, finely chopped
- 2 teaspoons capers, finely chopped
- Salt and ground black pepper, as required
- ¼ cup extra-virgin olive oil
- 1 teaspoon fresh lemon zest, finely grated
- ½ teaspoon garlic, finely chopped

Directions:

1. Preheat the Air fryer to 390 degrees F and grease an Air fryer basket.
2. Season the scallops evenly with salt and black pepper.
3. Arrange the scallops in the Air fryer basket and cook for about 6 minutes.

4. Mix parsley, capers, olive oil, lemon zest and garlic in a bowl.
5. Dish out the scallops in a platter and top with capers sauce.

Nutrition:

Calories: 344, Fat: 26.3g, Carbohydrates: 4.2g, Sugar: 0.1g, Protein: 24g, Sodium: 393mg

Crab Cakes

Preparation Time: 20 minutes

Cooking Time: 20 minutes

Servings: 4

Ingredients:

- 1 pound lump crab meat

- 1/3 cup panko breadcrumbs
- ¼ cup scallion, finely chopped
- 2 large eggs
- 1 teaspoon Dijon mustard
- 2 tablespoons mayonnaise
- 1 teaspoon Worcestershire sauce
- 1½ teaspoons Old Bay seasoning
- Ground black pepper, as required

Directions:

1. Preheat the Air fryer to 375 degrees F and grease an Air fryer basket.
2. Mix all the ingredients in a large bowl and cover to refrigerate for about 1 hour.
3. Make 8 equal-sized patties from the mixture and transfer 4 patties into the Air fryer.
4. Cook for about 10 minutes, flipping once in between and repeat with the remaining patties.
5. Dish out and serve warm.

Nutrition:

Calories: 183, Fat: 14.8g, Carbohydrates: 5.9g, Sugar: 1.1g, Protein: 20.1g, Sodium: 996mg

Delicious Shrimp recipe

Preparation Time: 17 minutes

Servings: 4

Ingredients:

- 1 lb. medium shelled and deveined shrimp
- 2 tbsp. sriracha
- ¼ cup full-fat mayonnaise
- 2 tbsp. salted butter; melted.
- ¼ tsp. garlic powder.
- ¼ tsp. powdered erythritol
- ⅛ tsp. ground black pepper
- ½ tsp. Old Bay seasoning

Directions:

1. Take a large bowl, toss shrimp in butter, Old Bay seasoning and garlic powder. Place shrimp into the air fryer basket
2. Adjust the temperature to 400 Degrees F and set the timer for 7 minutes.
3. Flip the shrimp halfway through the cooking time. Shrimp will be bright pink when fully cooked

4. In another large bowl, mix sriracha, powdered erythritol, mayonnaise and pepper.
5. Toss shrimp in the spicy mixture and serve immediately.

Nutrition:

Calories: 143; Protein: 16.4g; Fiber: 0.0g; Fat: 6.4g; Mg; Carbs: 3.0g

Lemon Fish

Preparation time: 30 minutes

Servings: 4

Ingredients:

- Water: .5 cup + 3 tbsp.
- Sugar: .25 cup
- Green chili sauce: 2 tsp.
- Juice of 1 lemon
- Salt: to your liking
- Egg white: 1
- Red chili sauce: 1 tsp.
- Corn flour slurry: 4 tsp.
- Lettuce: 2-3 leaves
- Catfish: 2 - cut into 4 pieces
- Oil: 2 tsp.

Directions:

1. Boil the water and sugar in a saucepan. Slice the lemon and place it in a dish.
2. Add the egg white, oil, chili sauce, salt, and flour in a bowl, mixing well. Add three tablespoons of water and whisk to make a smooth slurry batter.

3. Sprinkle flour onto a plate. Dip in the batter and then the flour.
4. Lightly grease the Air Fryer basket with a spritz of cooking oil spray and heat to reach 356º Fahrenheit.
5. Arrange the fillets in the basket and cook for 15 to 20 minutes until crispy.
6. Add salt to the pan and stir well. Add the corn flour slurry and remix it. Blend in the red sauce juice, and lemon slices, mixing well and cooking until thickened.
7. Remove the fish from the basket, brush with a spritz of oil, and place back into the pan. Cook for about five additional minutes.
8. Tear the leaves apart to make a serving bed. Add the fish and pour the lemon sauce over the top of the fish. Serve.

Tomato & Basil Scallops

Preparation time: 20 minutes

Servings: 2

Ingredients:

- Jumbo sea scallops: 8
- Vegetable oil to spray: as needed
- Frozen spinach: 12 oz.
- Tomato paste: 1 tbsp.
- Heavy whipping cream: .75 cup
- Chopped fresh basil: 1 tbsp.
- Minced garlic: 1 tsp.
- Black pepper & salt: .5 tsp. each
- Also Needed: 7-inch heat-proof pan
- Additional salt and pepper - to season scallops

Directions:

1. Thaw and drain the spinach.
2. Spray the pan. Scoop a layer of spinach in the pan.
3. Spray both sides of the scallops with vegetable oil. Dust with pepper and salt. Arrange the scallops in the pan on top of the spinach.

4. Combine the basil, garlic, cream, tomato paste, salt, and pepper. Pour the mixture over the spinach and scallops.
5. Set the Air Fryer at 350º Fahrenheit for 10 minutes until the scallops are cooked thoroughly. The sauce will also be bubbling.
6. Serve immediately.

Shrimp and Spaghetti

Preparation Time: 20 minutes

Servings: 4

Ingredients:

- 1 lb. shrimp; cooked, peeled and deveined
- 10 oz. canned tomatoes; chopped.
- 1 cup parmesan cheese; grated
- 1/4 tsp. oregano; dried
- 2 tbsp. olive oil

- 12 oz. spaghetti; cooked
- 1 garlic clove; minced
- 1 tbsp. parsley; finely chopped.

Directions:

1. In a pan that fits your air fryer, add the shrimp with the oil, garlic, tomatoes, oregano and parsley; toss well.
2. Place the pan in the fryer and cook at 380°F for 10 minutes
3. Add the spaghetti and the parmesan; toss well. Divide between plates, serve and enjoy!

Duck Breast with Figs

Preparation Time: 20 minutes

Cooking Time: 45 minutes

Servings: 2

Ingredients:

- 1 pound boneless duck breast
- 1 tablespoon fresh thyme, chopped
- 6 fresh figs, halved
- 2 cups fresh pomegranate juice
- 3 tablespoons brown sugar
- 2 tablespoons lemon juice
- 1 teaspoon olive oil
- Salt and black pepper, as required

Directions:

1. Preheat the Air fryer to 400 degrees F and grease an Air fryer basket.
2. Put the pomegranate juice, lemon juice, and brown sugar in a medium saucepan over medium heat.
3. Bring to a boil and simmer on low heat for about 25 minutes.

4. Season the duck breasts generously with salt and black pepper.
5. Arrange the duck breasts into the Air fryer basket, skin side up and cook for about 14 minutes, flipping once in between.
6. Dish out the duck breasts onto a cutting board for about 10 minutes.
7. Meanwhile, put the figs, olive oil, salt, and black pepper in a bowl until well mixed.
8. Set the Air fryer to 400 degrees F and arrange the figs into the Air fryer basket.
9. Cook for about 5 more minutes and dish out in a platter.
10. Put the duck breast with the roasted figs and drizzle with warm pomegranate juice mixture.
11. Garnish with fresh thyme and serve warm.

Nutrition:

Calories: 699, Fat: 12.1g, Carbohydrates: 90g, Sugar: 74g, Protein: 519g, Sodium: 110mg

Gyro Seasoned Chicken

Preparation Time: 10 minutes

Cooking Time: 30 minutes

Servings: 4

Ingredients:

- 2 pounds chicken thighs
- 2 tablespoons primal palate super gyro seasoning
- 1 tablespoon avocado oil
- 2 tablespoons primal palate new bae seasoning
- 1 tablespoon Himalayan pink salt

Directions:

1. Preheat the Air fryer to 350 degrees F and grease an Air fryer basket.
2. Rub the chicken with avocado oil and half of the spices.
3. Arrange the chicken thighs in the Air fryer basket and cook for about 25 minutes, flipping once in between.

4. Sprinkle the remaining seasoning and cook for 5 more minutes.
5. Dish out and serve warm.

Nutrition:

Calories: 545, Fat: 36.4g, Carbohydrates: 0.7g, Sugar: 0g, Protein: 42.5g, Sodium: 272mg

Chicken and Yogurt

Preparation Time: 1 hour 15 minutes

Servings: 4

Ingredients:

- 17 oz. chicken meat; boneless and cubed
- 14 oz. yogurt
- 1 red bell pepper; deseeded and cubed
- 3½ oz. cherry tomatoes; halved
- 1 yellow bell pepper; deseeded and cubed
- 2 tbsp. coriander powder
- 1 tsp. turmeric powder
- 2 tsp. olive oil
- 3 mint leaves; torn
- 1 green bell pepper; deseeded and cubed
- 1 tbsp. ginger; grated
- 2 tbsp. red chili powder
- 2 tbsp. cumin powder
- Salt and black pepper to taste

Directions:

1. In a bowl, mix all of the ingredients, toss well and place in the fridge for 1 hour
2. Transfer the whole mix to a pan that fits your air fryer and cook at 400 °F for 15 minutes, shaking the pan halfway. Divide everything between plates and serve

Chicken and Baby Carrots

Preparation Time: 35 minutes

Servings: 4

Ingredients:

- 6 chicken thighs
- 1/2 lb. baby carrots; halved
- 15 oz. canned tomatoes; chopped.
- 1 cup chicken stock
- 1 yellow onion; chopped.
- 1 tsp. olive oil

- 1/2 tsp. thyme; dried
- 2 tbsp. tomato paste
- 1/2 cup white wine
- Salt and black pepper to taste

Directions:

1. Put the oil into a pan that fits your air fryer and heat up over medium heat.
2. Add the chicken thighs and brown them for 1-2 minutes on each side
3. Add all the remaining ingredients, toss and cook for 4-5 minutes more
4. Place the pan in the air fryer and cook at 380°F for 22 minutes. Divide the chicken and carrots mix between plates and serve.

Chicken Fajita Casserole

Preparation Time: 10 minutes

Cooking Time: 12 minutes

Serve: 4

Ingredients:

- 1 lb cooked chicken, shredded
- 1 onion, sliced
- 1 bell pepper, sliced
- 1/3 cup mayonnaise
- 7 oz cream cheese
- 7 oz cheese, shredded
- 2 tbsp tex-mex seasoning
- Pepper
- Salt

Directions:

1. Preheat the air fryer to 370 F.
2. Spray air fryer baking dish with cooking spray.
3. Mix all ingredients except 2 oz shredded cheese in a prepared dish.

4. Spread remaining cheese on top.
5. Place dish in the air fryer and cook for 12 minutes.
6. Serve and enjoy.

Nutrition:

Calories 640, Fat 43.8 g, Carbohydrates 11 g, Sugar 4.3 g, Protein 50 g, Cholesterol 200 mg

Rotisserie Chicken

Cooking Time: 1 hour

Servings: 4

Ingredients:

- 1 to 2 tbsp. ghee or preferred oil
- 1 whole chicken; cleaned and blotted dry.
- 1 tbsp. seasoning salt

Directions:

1. Rub your chosen oil all over the chicken and season generously. Place it breast-side own on the air fryer and cook at 350°F for 30 minutes. Flip the chicken over and cook for another 30 minutes, or until it reaches 165°F. Let it rest for 10 minutes and serve

Mustard Lamb Loin Chops

Preparation Time: 15 minutes

Cooking Time: 30 minutes

Servings: 4

Ingredients:

- 8: 4-ounceslamb loin chops
- 1 tablespoon fresh lemon juice
- 2 tablespoons Dijon mustard

- 1 teaspoon dried tarragon
- ½ teaspoon olive oil
- Salt and black pepper, to taste

Directions:

1. Preheat the Air fryer to 390 degrees F and grease an Air fryer basket.
2. Mix the mustard, lemon juice, oil, tarragon, salt, and black pepper in a large bowl.
3. Coat the chops generously with the mustard mixture and arrange in the Air fryer basket.
4. Cook for about 15 minutes, flipping once in between and dish out to serve hot.

Nutrition:

Calories: 433, Fat: 17.6g, Carbohydrates: 0.6g, Sugar: 0.2g, Protein: 64.1g, Sodium: 201mg

Leg of Lamb with Brussels Sprout

Preparation Time: 20 minutes

Cooking Time: 1 hour 30 minutes

Servings: 6

Ingredients:

- 2¼ pounds leg of lamb
- 1 tablespoon fresh rosemary, minced
- 1½ pounds Brussels sprouts, trimmed
- 1 tablespoon fresh lemon thyme
- 3 tablespoons olive oil, divided
- Salt and ground black pepper, as required
- 1 garlic clove, minced
- 2 tablespoons honey

Directions:

1. Preheat the Air fryer to 300 degrees F and grease an Air fryer basket.
2. Make slits in the leg of lamb with a sharp knife.
3. Mix 2 tablespoons of oil, herbs, garlic, salt, and black pepper in a bowl.

4. Coat the leg of lamb with oil mixture generously and arrange in the Air fryer basket.
5. Cook for about 75 minutes and set the Air fryer to 390 degrees F.
6. Coat the Brussels sprout evenly with the remaining oil and honey and arrange them in the Air fryer basket with the leg of lamb.
7. Cook for about 15 minutes and dish out to serve warm.

Nutrition:

Calories: 449, Fats: 19.9g, Carbohydrates: 16.6g, Sugar: 8.2g, Proteins: 51.7g, Sodium: 185mg

Beef Pot Pie

Preparation Time: 10 minutes

Cooking Time: 1 hour 27 minutes

Servings: 3

Ingredients:

- 1 pound beef stewing steak, cubed
- 1 can ale mixed into 1 cup water
- 1 tablespoon plain flour
- 2 beef bouillon cubes
- 1 prepared short crust pastry
- 1 tablespoon tomato puree
- 1 tablespoon olive oil
- 2 tablespoons onion paste
- Salt and black pepper, to taste

Directions:

1. Preheat the Air fryer to 390 degrees F and grease 2 ramekins lightly.
2. Heat olive oil in a pan and add steak cubes.
3. Cook for about 5 minutes and stir in the onion paste and tomato puree.

4. Cook for about 6 minutes and add the ale mixture, bouillon cubes, salt and black pepper.
5. Bring to a boil and reduce the heat to simmer for about 1 hour.
6. Mix flour and 3 tablespoons of warm water in a bowl and slowly add this mixture into the beef mixture.
7. Roll out the short crust pastry and line 2 ramekins with pastry.
8. Divide the beef mixture evenly in the ramekins and top with extra pastry.
9. Transfer into the Air fryer and cook for about 10 minutes.
10. Set the Air fryer to 335 ^{0}F and cook for about 6 more minutes.
11. Dish out and serve warm.

Nutrition:

Calories: 442, Fat: 14.2g, Carbohydrates: 19g, Sugar: 1.2g, Protein: 50.6g, Sodium: 583mg

Five Spice Pork

Preparation Time: 15 minutes

Cooking Time: 20 minutes

Servings: 4

Ingredients:

- 1-pound pork belly
- 2 tablespoons swerve
- 1 tablespoon Shaoxing: cooking wine
- 2 tablespoons dark soy sauce
- 2 teaspoons garlic, minced
- 1 tablespoon hoisin sauce
- 2 teaspoons ginger, minced
- 1 teaspoon Chinese Five Spice

Directions:

1. Preheat the Air fryer to 390 degrees F and grease an Air fryer basket.
2. Mix all the ingredients in a bowl and place in the Ziplock bag.
3. Seal the bag, shake it well and refrigerate to marinate for about 1 hour.

4. Remove the pork from the bag and arrange it in the Air fryer basket.
5. Cook for about 15 minutes and dish out in a bowl to serve warm.

Nutrition:

Calories: 604, Fat: 30.6g, Carbohydrates: 1.4g, Sugar: 20.3g, Protein: 19.8g, Sodium: 834mg

Beef Roast

Preparation Time: 65 minutes

Servings: 4

Ingredients:

- 2 lbs. beef roast
- 3 tbsp. garlic; minced
- 1 tbsp. smoked paprika
- 3 tbsp. olive oil
- Salt and black pepper to taste

Directions:

1. In a bowl, combine all the ingredients and coat the roast well.
2. Place the roast in your air fryer and cook at 390 °F for 55 minutes. Slice the roast, divide it between plates and serve with a side salad

Paprika Beef

Preparation Time: 30 minutes

Servings: 4

Ingredients:

- 1½ lbs. beef fillet
- 1 red onion; roughly chopped.
- 1 tbsp. tomato paste
- 1 tbsp. Worcestershire sauce
- 1/2 cup beef stock
- 3 tsp. sweet paprika
- 2 tbsp. olive oil
- Salt and black pepper to taste

Directions:

1. In a bowl, mix the beef with all remaining ingredients; toss well.
2. Transfer the mixture to a pan that fits your air fryer and cook at 400 °F for 26 minutes, shaking the air fryer halfway. Divide everything between plates and serve

Pork Spare Ribs

Servings: 6

Preparation Time: 15 minutes

Cooking Time: 20 minutes

Ingredients

- 5-6 garlic cloves, minced
- ½ cup rice vinegar
- 2 tablespoons soy sauce
- Salt and ground black pepper, as required
- 12: 1-inchpork spare ribs
- ½ cup cornstarch
- 2 tablespoons olive oil

Directions:

1. In a large bowl, mix the garlic, vinegar, soy sauce, salt, and black pepper.
2. Add the ribs and generously coat with mixture.
3. Refrigerate to marinate overnight.
4. In a shallow bowl, place the cornstarch.
5. Coat the ribs evenly with cornstarch and then drizzle with oil.
6. Set the temperature of air fryer to 390 degrees

F. Grease an air fryer basket.

7. Arrange ribs into the prepared air fryer basket in a single layer.
8. Air fry for about 10 minutes per side.
9. Remove from air fryer and transfer the ribs onto serving plates.
10. Serve immediately.

Nutrition:

Calories: 557, Carbohydrate: 11g, Protein: 35g, Fat: 51.3g, Sugar: 0.1g, Sodium: 997mg

Garlic Lamb Roast

Servings: 6

Preparation Time: 20 minutes

Cooking Time: 1½ hours

Ingredients

- 2¾ pounds half lamb leg roast
- 2 tablespoons extra-virgin olive oil
- 3 garlic cloves, cut into thin slices
- 1 tablespoon dried rosemary, crushed
- Salt and ground black pepper, as required

Directions:

1. In a small bowl, mix together the oil, rosemary, salt, and black pepper.
2. With the tip of a sharp knife, make deep slits on the top of lamb roast fat.
3. Insert the garlic slices into the slits.
4. Coat the lamb roast evenly with oil mixture.
5. Set the temperature of air fryer to 390 degrees F. Grease an air fryer basket.
6. Arrange lamb into the prepared air fryer basket in a single layer.

7. Air Fry for about 15 minutes and then another 1¼ hours at 320 degrees F.
8. Remove from air fryer and transfer the roast onto a platter.
9. With a piece of foil, cover the roast for about 10 minutes before slicing.
10. Cut the roast into desired size slices and serve.

Nutrition:

Calories: 418, Carbohydrate: 0.9g, Protein: 57.4g, Fat: 14.9g, Sugar: 0g ,Sodium: 165mg

Veal, speck, and cheese paupiettes

Preparation time: 10-20 minutes,

Cooking time: 15-30 minutes;

Serve: 6

Ingredients

- 12 slices of veal
- 6 speck slices

- 12 slices of provola
- Salt to taste
- Pepper to taste

Directions:

1. Place half a slice of stain and one of provola on each slice of veal; Roll each slice and close them with toothpicks.
2. Pour the oil and place the paupiettes in the basket, season with salt and pepper.
3. Set the air fryer to 180 ºC.
4. Cook the paupiettes for 15 minutes, turning them around after about 8 to 9 minutes.

Nutrition:

Calories 261, Carbohydrates 0g, Fat 11g, Sugar 0g, Protein 30g, Cholesterol 0mg

Broccoli Crust Pizza

Preparation Time: 27 minutes

Servings: 4

Ingredients:

- 3 cups riced broccoli, steamed and drained well
- ½ cup shredded mozzarella cheese
- ½ cup grated vegetarian Parmesan cheese.
- 1 large egg.
- 3 tbsp. low-carb Alfredo sauce

Directions:

1. Take a large bowl, mix broccoli, egg and Parmesan.
2. Cut a piece of parchment to fit your air fryer basket. Press out the pizza mixture to fit on the parchment, working in two batches if necessary. Place into the air fryer basket. Adjust the temperature to 370 Degrees F and set the timer for 5 minutes.
3. When the timer beeps, the crust should be firm enough to flip. If not, add 2 additional minutes. Flip crust.

4. Top with Alfredo sauce and mozzarella. Return to the air fryer basket and cook an additional 7 minutes or until cheese is golden and bubbling. Serve warm.

Nutrition:

Calories: 136; Protein: 9.9g; Fiber: 2.3g; Fat: 7.6g; Carbs:5.7g

Beef Noodle Soup

Preparation Time: 8 minutes

Cooking Time: 35 minutes

Servings: 4

Ingredients:

- ½ lb of beef shoulder
- 1 Tbsp of kosher salt
- ¼ Cup of fresh ground black pepper
- ¼ Teaspoon of ground ginger
- ½ Teaspoon of all spice

- 1 Tbsp of coconut oil
- 4 Cups of chicken broth
- 1 Piece of 1 inch of fresh ginger
- ¼ Cups of fish sauce
- 1 Medium head of bok choy
- 1 or 2 packages of Shriataki noodles
- 1 Head of cabbage
- 2 scallions
- ¼ Cup of cilantro
- 1 Cup of bean sprouts

Directions:

1. Cut the beef into one and small cubes of 1 inch each.
2. Blend all together the salt, the pepper, the all spice powder and the ginger.
3. Spice the quantity of beef cubes into the mixture of the spices.
4. Put the air fryer to the feature sauté, and once it becomes hot; then stir in the beef and sauté it until it becomes brown.
5. Add the broth of chicken
6. Add the fish sauce and the ginger

7. Now, lock the lid over the Air fryer and Put the air fryer to the Beef. Feature Stew and cook it for around 30 minutes. Meanwhile; cut the bok choy, the Napa cabbage and the scallions

8. When the cooking process is complete and the Air fryer's timer gets off, vent your steam and remove its lid. Then set the feature of the Air fryer to the mode sauté

9. Add the Napa cabbage, the bok choy and the scallion; then simmer for around 5 minutes

10. Drain your noodles and rinse it; then add it to your air fryer. Let the ingredients simmer for around 2 minutes

11. Serve and enjoy your soup with cilantro for garnish and sprouts

Nutrition:

Calories – 204.4 Protein – 11.7 g. Fat – 7.5 g. Carbs – 27.8 g.

Tortilla and White Beans Soup

Preparation Time: 10 minutes

Cooking Time: 27 minutes

Servings: 4

Ingredients:

- 1 cup white beans
- 4 tablespoons butter
- ¼ teaspoon white pepper
- 1 onion, roughly sliced
- 1 tablespoon sun dried tomatoes
- ¼ cup fresh cream
- 4 cups water
- 2 teaspoons salt
- 1 carrot, roughly chopped
- 4 garlic cloves, minced
- 4 tablespoons tomato paste
- Crunchy tortilla chips, for garnish

Directions:

1. Put the butter, garlic, carrots, onions and white pepper in the Air fryer and select "Sauté".

2. Sauté for 5 minutes and add white beans, potatoes, sun dried tomatoes, tomato paste, salt and water.
3. Set the Air fryer to "Soup" and cook for 12 minutes at high pressure.
4. Release the pressure naturally and add sour cream.
5. Blend the contents of the Air fryer to a smooth consistency and top with crunchy tortilla chips.

Nutrition:

Calories: 353; Total Fat: 14.7g; Carbs: 44.2g; Sugars: 5.3g; Protein: 14g

Chestnut Soup

Preparation Time: 10 minutes

Cooking Time: 25 minutes

Servings: 4

Ingredients:

- ½ pound fresh chestnuts
- 1 sprig sage
- 4 tablespoons butter
- ¼ teaspoon white pepper
- ¼ teaspoon nutmeg
- 1 stalk celery, chopped
- 1 onion, chopped
- 1 potato, chopped
- 2 tablespoons rum
- 2 tablespoons fresh cream

Directions:

1. Puree the fresh chestnuts in a blender.
2. Put the butter, onions, sage, celery and white pepper in the Air fryer and select "Sauté".

3. Sauté for 4 minutes and add potato, stock and chestnuts.
4. Set the Air fryer to "Soup" and cook for 15 minutes at high pressure.
5. Release the pressure naturally and add rum, nutmeg and fresh cream.
6. Blend the contents of the Air fryer to a smooth consistency.

Nutrition:

Calories: 290; Total Fat: 13.3g; Carbs: 36.5g; Sugars: 2.5g; Protein: 3g

Pearl Barley Soup

Preparation Time: 10 minutes

Cooking Time: 25 minutes

Servings: 66

Ingredients:

- 1 cup all-purpose flour
- 2 celery stalks, chopped
- 2 onions, chopped
- 2 carrots, chopped
- 4 tablespoons olive oil
- 28 oz. vegetable stock
- 2 cups mushroom, sliced
- ¾ cup pearl barley
- 2 teaspoons dried oregano
- 1 cup purple wine
- Salt and pepper, to taste

Directions:

1. Put the oil, garlic and onions in the Air fryer and select "Sauté".

2. Sauté for 3 minutes and add rest of the ingredients.
3. Set the Air fryer to "Soup" and cook for 15 minutes at high pressure.
4. Release the pressure naturally and serve hot.

Nutrition:

Calories: 310;Total Fat: 10.1g;Carbs: 43.8g; Sugars: 4.2g; Protein: 6.6g

Bacon Wrapped Onion Rings.

Preparation Time: 15 minutes

Servings: 4

Ingredients:

- 1 large onion; peeled.
- 8 slices sugar-free bacon.
- 1 tbsp. sriracha

Directions:

1. Slice onion into ¼-inch-thick slices. Brush sriracha over the onion slices. Take two slices of onion and wrap bacon around the rings. Repeat with remaining onion and bacon
2. Place into the air fryer basket. Adjust the temperature to 350 Degrees F and set the timer for 10 minutes.
3. Use tongs to flip the onion rings halfway through the cooking time. When fully cooked, bacon will be crispy. Serve warm

Nutrition:

Calories: 105; Protein: 7.5g; Fiber: 0.6g; Fat: 5.9g; Carbs: 4.3g

Parmesan Chicken Wings

Preparation Time: 30 minutes

Servings: 4

Ingredients:

- 2 lb. raw chicken wings
- ⅓ cup grated Parmesan cheese.
- 4 tbsp. unsalted butter; melted.
- 1 tbsp. baking powder
- ¼ tsp. dried parsley.
- ½ tsp. garlic powder.
- 1 tsp. pink Himalayan salt

Directions:

1. Take a large bowl, place chicken wings, salt, ½ tsp. garlic powder. and baking powder, then toss. Place wings into the air fryer basket
2. Adjust the temperature to 400 Degrees F and set the timer for 25 minutes. Toss the basket two or three times during the cooking time
3. In a small bowl, combine butter, Parmesan and parsley.

4. Remove wings from the fryer and place into a clean large bowl. Pour the butter mixture over the wings and toss until coated. Serve warm.

Nutrition:

Calories: 565; Protein: 41.8g; Fiber: 0.1g; Fat: 42.1g; Carbs: 2.2g

Sponge Ricotta Cake

Preparation Time: 35 minutes

Servings: 8

Ingredients:

- 3 eggs, whisked
- 1 cup almond flour
- 1 cup ricotta, soft
- 7 tbsp. ghee; melted
- 1/3 swerve
- 1 tsp. baking powder
- Cooking spray

Directions:

1. In a bowl, combine all the ingredients except the cooking spray and stir them very well.
2. Grease a cake pan that fits the air fryer with the cooking spray and pour the cake mix inside.
3. Put the pan in the fryer and cook at 350°F for 30 minutes
4. Cool the cake down, slice and serve.

Nutrition:

Calories: 210; Fat: 12g; Fiber: 3g; Carbs: 6g; Protein: 9g

Lemon Blackberries Cake

Preparation Time: 35 minutes

Servings: 4

Ingredients:

- 2 eggs, whisked
- ¼ cup almond milk
- 1 ½ cups almond flour
- 1 cup blackberries; chopped.

- 2 tbsp. ghee; melted
- 1 tsp. lemon zest, grated
- 1 tsp. lemon juice
- 4 tbsp. swerve
- ½ tsp. baking powder

Directions:

1. Take a bowl and mix all the ingredients and whisk well.
2. Pour this into a cake pan that fits the air fryer lined with parchment paper, put the pan in your air fryer and cook at 340 °F for 25 minutes. Cool the cake down, slice and serve

Nutrition:

Calories: 193; Fat: 5g; Fiber: 1g; Carbs: 4g; Protein: 4g

Lemon Bars

Preparation Time: 10 minutes

Cooking time: 35 minutes

Servings: 8

Ingredients:

- ½ cup butter, melted
- 1 cup erythritol
- 3 eggs, whisked
- 1 and ¾ cups almond flour
- Zest of 1 lemon, grated
- Juice of 3 lemons

Directions:

1. In a bowl, mix 1 cup flour with half of the erythritol and the butter, stir well and press into a baking dish that fits the air fryer lined with parchment paper.
2. Put the dish in your air fryer and cook at 350 degrees F for 10 minutes.
3. Meanwhile, in a bowl, mix the rest of the flour with the remaining erythritol and the other Ingredients: and whisk well.

4. Spread this over the crust, put the dish in the air fryer once more and cook at 350 degrees F for 25 minutes.
5. Cool down, cut into bars and serve.

Nutrition:

Calories 210, fat 12, fiber 1, carbs 4, protein 8

Coconut Cookies

Preparation Time: 5 minutes

Cooking time: 15 minutes

Servings: 8

Ingredients:

- 1 and ½ cups coconut, shredded
- ½ teaspoon baking powder
- 2 tablespoons erythritol

- ¼ teaspoon almond extract
- 2 eggs, whisked

Directions:

1. In a bowl, mix all the Ingredients: and whisk well.
2. Scoop 8 servings of this mix on a baking sheet that fits the air fryer which you've lined with parchment paper.
3. Put the baking sheet in your air fryer and cook at 350 degrees F for 15 minutes.
4. Serve cold.

Nutrition:

Calories 125, fat 7, fiber 1, carbs 5, protein 4

Chocolaty Squares

Preparation Time: 15 minutes

Cooking Time: 20 minutes

Servings: 4

Ingredients:

- 2-ounce cold butter
- 3-ounce self-rising flour

- ½ tablespoon milk
- 2-ounce chocolate, chopped
- 1¼-ounce brown sugar
- 1/8 cup honey

Directions:

1. Preheat the Air fryer to 320 degrees F and grease a tin lightly.
2. Mix butter, brown sugar, flour and honey and beat till smooth.
3. Stir in the chocolate and milk and pour the mixture into a tin.
4. Transfer into the Air fryer basket and cook for about 20 minutes.
5. Dish out and cut into desired squares to serve.

Nutrition:

Calories: 322, Fat: 15.9g, Carbohydrates: 42.2g, Sugar: 24.8g, Protein: 3.5g, Sodium: 97mg

Cherry Pie

Preparation Time: 20 minutes

Cooking Time: 15 minutes

Servings: 4

Ingredients:

- ½: 21-ouncecan cherry pie filling
- 1 refrigerated pre-made pie crust
- ½ tablespoon milk
- 1 egg yolk

- 1 tablespoon vegetable oil

Directions:

1. Preheat the Air fryer to 320 degrees F and press pie crust into a pie pan.
2. Poke the holes with a fork all over the dough and transfer the pie pan into the Air fryer basket.
3. Cook for about 5 minutes and remove from the Air fryer.
4. Pour the cherry pie filling into pie crust.
5. Cut the remaining pie crust into ¾-inch strips and place the strips in a crisscrossing manner.
6. Whisk egg and milk in a small bowl and brush the egg wash on the top of pie.
7. Transfer the pie pan into the Air fryer basket and cook for about 15 minutes to serve.

Nutrition:

Calories: 307, Fat: 1.4g, Carbohydrates: 70g, Sugar: 57.9g, Protein: 1g, Sodium: 130mg

Pear Delight

Preparation Time: 25 minutes

Servings: 4

Ingredients:

- 4 pears; peeled and roughly cut into cubes
- 1/4 cup brown sugar
- 4 tbsp. butter; melted
- 2 tsp. cinnamon powder
- 1 tbsp. maple syrup

Directions:

1. In a pan that fits your air fryer, place all the ingredients and toss.
2. Place the pan in the air fryer and cook at 300 °F for 20 minutes. Divide into cups, refrigerate and serve cold

Butter Donuts

Preparation Time: 25 minutes

Servings: 4

Ingredients:

- 8 oz. flour
- 4 oz. whole milk
- 2½ tbsp. butter
- 1 egg
- 1 tbsp. brown sugar
- 1 tbsp. white sugar
- 1 tsp. baking powder

Directions:

1. Place all of the ingredients in a bowl and mix well.
2. Shape donuts from this mix and place them in your air fryer's basket
3. Cook at 360 °F for 15 minutes. Arrange the donuts on a platter and serve them warm

Brioche Pudding

Preparation Time: 35 minutes

Servings: 4

Ingredients:

- 3 cups brioche; cubed
- 2 cups half and half
- 1/2 tsp. vanilla extract
- 2 cups milk
- 1/2 cup raisins
- 4 egg yolks; whisked
- 1 cup sugar
- 2 tbsp. butter; melted
- Zest of 1/2 lemon

Directions:

1. In a bowl, add all of the ingredients and whisk well
2. Pour the mixture into a pudding mould and place it in the air fryer
3. Cook at 330 °F for 30 minutes. Cool down and serve.

Lusciously Easy Brownies

Servings: 8

Cooking Time: 20 minutes

Ingredients

- 1 egg
- 2 tablespoons and 2 teaspoons unsweetened cocoa powder
- 1/2 teaspoon vanilla extract
- 1/2 cup white sugar
- 1/4 cup butter
- 1/4 cup all-purpose flour
- 1/8 teaspoon salt
- 1/8 teaspoon baking powder

Frosting Ingredients

- 1 tablespoon and 1-1/2 teaspoons butter, softened
- 1 tablespoon and 1-1/2 teaspoons unsweetened cocoa powder
- 1-1/2 teaspoons honey
- 1/2 teaspoon vanilla extract
- 1/2 cup confectioners' sugar

Directions:

1. Lightly grease baking pan of air fryer with cooking spray. Melt ¼ cup butter for 3 minutes. Stir in vanilla, eggs, and sugar. Mix well.
2. Stir in baking powder, salt, flour, and cocoa mix well. Evenly spread.
3. For 20 minutes, cook on 300oF.
4. In a small bowl, make the frosting by mixing well all Ingredients. Frost brownies while still warm.
5. Serve and enjoy.

Nutrition:

Calories: 191; Carbs: 25.7g; Protein: 1.8g; Fat: 9.0g

Espresso Mini Cheesecake

Preparation Time: 20 minutes

Servings: 2

Ingredients:

- ½ cup walnuts
- 1 large egg.
- 4 oz. full-fat cream cheese; softened.
- 2 tbsp. salted butter
- 2 tbsp. granular erythritol.
- 2 tbsp. powdered erythritol
- 1 tsp. espresso powder
- ½ tsp. vanilla extract.
- 2 tsp. unsweetened cocoa powder

Directions:

1. Place walnuts, butter and granular erythritol in a food processor. Pulse until ingredients stick together and a dough forms.
2. Press dough into 4-inch springform pan and place into the air fryer basket.
3. Adjust the temperature to 400 Degrees F and set the timer for 5 minutes. When the timer

beeps, remove crust and let cool.

4. Take a medium bowl, mix cream cheese with egg, vanilla extract, powdered erythritol, cocoa powder and espresso powder until smooth.

5. Spoon mixture on top of baked walnut crust and place into the air fryer basket. Adjust the temperature for 300 Degrees F and set the timer for 10 minutes. Once done, chill for 2 hours before serving.

Nutrition:

Calories: 535; Protein: 11.6g; Fiber: 7.2g; Fat: 48.4g; Carbs: 37.1g

Notes

www.ingramcontent.com/pod-product-compliance
Lightning Source LLC
Chambersburg PA
CBHW070933080526
44589CB00013B/1499